Behold, I Stand at the Door and Knock

Behold, I Stand at the Door and Knock

TRACY CAROL TAYLOR

PRINCE OF PAGES, INC.
ARLINGTON

Behold, I Stand at the Door and Knock

Copyright © 2019 by Tracy Carol Taylor. All Rights Reserved.

No part of this publication may be reproduced, stored in a retrieval system or transmitted in any way by any means, electronic, mechanical, photocopy, recording, or otherwise without the proper permission of the author except as provided by USA copyright law.

Scripture quotations marked (KJV) are taken from the Holy Bible, King James Version, Cambridge, 1769. Used by permission. All rights reserved.

Scripture quotations marked (NIV) are taken from the Holy Bible, New International Version, NIV, Copyright © 1973, 1978, 1984 by Biblica, Inc. TM Used by permission of Zondervan. All rights reserved worldwide. www.zondervan.com

The Holy Bible, International Children's Bible® Copyright© 1986, 1988, 1999, 2015 by Tommy Nelson™, a division of Thomas Nelson. Used by permission.

The opinions expressed by the author are not necessarily those of Prince of Pages, Inc.

Published by Prince of Pages, Inc.
Carlin Springs Road | Arlington, VA 22203 USA
www.princeofpages.com

Cover design by Getty Images
Interior design by Pinterest
Published in the United States of America
ISBN: 978-1-949252-05-7

Religion, Children, Devotional
Religion, Christian Life, Personal Growth

Contents

Chapter 1	1
Chapter 2	8
Chapter 3	20
Chapter 4	27
Chapter 5	43
Chapter 6	46
Other Books by Author	57

Chapter 1

Behold, I Stand at the Door and Knock

19 As many as I love, I rebuke and chasten: be zealous therefore, and repent.

20 Behold, I stand at the door, and knock: if any man hear my voice, and open the door, I will come in to him, and will sup with him, and he with me.

21 To him that overcometh will I grant to sit with me in my throne, even as I also overcame, and am set down with my Father in his throne.

22 He that hath an ear, let him hear what the Spirit saith unto the churches.

Revelations 3:19-22 KJV

Jesus is waiting for us to open our hearts to him and his teachings. When I was a child, my Sunday school teacher explained that just as your friends will ring your doorbell when they visit, and you can choose whether or not to let them in; you can also choose whether or not to live for God. Jesus never forced anyone to obey him. He never forced anyone to do anything that they didn't want to do. You have a choice, just as people in the bible had a choice. They either chose to believe Jesus and listen to him or they chose to ignore him, and their lives remained unchanged.

Jesus Cleanses a Leper

40 And there came a leper to him, beseeching him, and kneeling down to him, and saying unto him, If thou wilt, thou canst make me clean.

41 And Jesus, moved with compassion, put forth his hand, and touched him, and saith unto him, I will; be thou clean.

42 And as soon as he had spoken, immediately the leprosy departed from him, and he was cleansed.

43 And he straitly charged him, and forthwith sent him away;

44 And saith unto him, See thou say nothing to any man: but go thy way, shew thyself to the priest, and offer for thy cleansing those things which Moses commanded, for a testimony unto them.

45 But he went out, and began to publish it much, and to blaze abroad the matter, insomuch that Jesus could no more openly enter into the city, but was without in desert places: and they came to him from every quarter.

Mark 1:40-45 KJV

Can you image what the leper's life would have continued to be like if he hadn't believed in Jesus.

Jesus Heals a Palsied Man

1 And he entered into a ship, and passed over, and came into his own city.

2 And, behold, they brought to him a man sick of the palsy, lying on a bed: and Jesus seeing their faith said unto the sick of the palsy; Son, be of good cheer; thy sins be forgiven thee.

3 And, behold, certain of the scribes said within themselves, This man blasphemeth.

4 And Jesus knowing their thoughts said, Wherefore think ye evil in your hearts?

5 For whether is easier, to say, Thy sins be forgiven thee; or to say, Arise, and walk?

6 But that ye may know that the Son of man hath power on earth to forgive sins, (then saith he to the sick of the palsy,) Arise, take up thy bed, and go unto thine house.

7 And he arose, and departed to his house.

8 But when the multitudes saw it, they marveled, and glorified God, which had given such power unto men.

Matthew 9:1-8 KJV

Again, what would this man's been like if he didn't choose to believe Jesus at his word. Jesus told him to take up his bed, and he did. He didn't argue. He didn't complain. He didn't say, "Um, Jesus, I don't know if you noticed, but my legs don't work." No. He chose to believe Jesus at his word, and he was healed. His life was changed for the better because he chose to believe in Jesus.

Jesus Heals the Man with the Withered Hand

10 And, behold, there was a man which had his hand withered. And they asked him, saying, Is it lawful to heal on the sabbath days? that they might accuse him.
11 And he said unto them, What man shall there be among you, that shall have one sheep, and if it fall into a pit on the sabbath day, will he not lay hold on it, and lift it out?
12 How much then is a man better than a sheep? Wherefore it is lawful to do well on the sabbath days.
13 Then saith he to the man, Stretch forth thine hand. And he stretched it forth; and it was restored whole, like as the other.
Matthew 12:10-13 KJV

The same is said for this person. He obeyed Jesus and he was healed. No one who chose to believe God at his word, has ever said that they regret it.

In fact, if I told you that you could have One Million dollars and all you had to do was three things, would you do it? Some people would jump at the chance. Others would think about it a bit and want more information. Still others would think that it was too good to be true or that I was lying and just ignore me. Losing out on one million dollars all because they were unwilling to believe.

Faith in God is often like that. Some people believe and live their lives according to God's commandments. Some don't believe right away, but will sometimes come around. Others strait out refuse to believe and laugh at others that do. Calling them stupid or dupes.

But you see just as we can be taught to trust, we can be taught to distrust as well. And unfortunately, bad people have taken their toll on our levels of trust. So much so, that when a good thing does come along, we are unwilling to believe it.

But the things of God are true. There is a

heaven. There is a hell. Man has a soul, and it will spend an eternity somewhere. And whether you believe it or not, does not negate that fact that it will happen.

Just because you've never seen a penguin does not mean that penguins do not exist. Just because you can't see the wind or a black hole, does not mean that they do not exist. They will affect you whether you believe in them or not.

But let me tell you why this is important. Let me tell you how all of this started. Let me tell you that Jesus wants to save your soul from hell and that he stands at the door and knocks. Question is…will you let him in.

Chapter 2

In the Beginning...

It all started when God made the angels. The angels were to be his messengers and praise singers. But one angel was made special and had the most beautiful voice in all the heavens. And his name was Lucifer. Lucifer was the number one choir singer. But he was also proud of himself. So proud in fact that he thought that he should replace God.

The Fall of Lucifer

12 "How art thou fallen from heaven, O Lucifer, son of the morning! how art thou cut down to the ground, which didst weaken the nations!

13 For thou hast said in thine heart, I will ascend into heaven, I will exalt my throne above the stars of God: I will sit also upon the mount of the congregation, in the sides of the north:

14 I will ascend above the heights of the clouds; I will be like the most High.

15 Yet thou shalt be brought down to hell, to the sides of the pit.

16 They that see thee shall narrowly look upon thee, and consider thee, saying, Is this the man that made the earth to tremble, that did shake kingdoms;

17 That made the world as a wilderness, and destroyed the cities thereof; that opened not the house of his prisoners?"

Isaiah 14:12-17 (King James Version – KJV)

Now, God did not like Lucifer's attitude of pride, and Lucifer was cast out of Heaven. Not only did Lucifer lose his place in Heaven, but he lost his name as well. No longer was he called Lucifer, morning star or bearer of light. Nope, now he was called Satan, and Satan means adversary.

Satan was now God's enemy and our adversary, but he was not going to go down alone. Have you ever been in trouble or you're angry at someone, and you know the best way to get back at them, is to hurt the person that they love the most. Well, that's just what Lucifer did. Satan took one-third of the angels with him. One-third of the angels that God had made, thought that Satan was right and sided with him. So, God kicked them all out too. Satan and his one-third were cast out of heaven and the angels lost their names and status as well. They are now called demons.

But that's not the end of this story, because this is where you come in. Well, I mean humanity. You see, Satan used to be the chief praise singer and worshiper. But God replaced Satan with humanity, and now all of us have been given that job of praise singer and worshiper. It is now humanity's job to be praising God and obeying his word.

God put man in the Garden of Eden. The most perfect place and he filled it with good things, and it was man's job to look after all of it. That's right the oldest profession in the world is Gardener. Think about that the next time you see a groundskeeper.

God Makes Man and Gives Him a Home

7 Then the Lord God took dust from the ground and formed man from it. The Lord

breathed the breath of life into the man's nose. And the man became a living person.

8 Then the Lord God planted a garden in the East, in a place called Eden. He put the man he had formed in that garden.

9 The Lord God caused every beautiful tree and every tree that was good for food to grow out of the ground. In the middle of the garden, God put the tree that gives life. And he put there the tree that gives the knowledge of good and evil.

10 A river flowed through Eden and watered the garden. From that point the river was divided. It had four streams flowing into it.

11 The name of the first stream is Pishon. It flows around the whole land of Havilah, where there is gold.

12 That gold is good. Bdellium and onyx are also there.

13 The name of the second river is Gihon. It flows around the whole land of Cush.

14 The name of the third river is Tigris. It flows out of Assyria toward the east. The fourth river is the Euphrates.

15 The Lord God put the man in the garden of Eden to care for it and work it.

16 The Lord God commanded him, "You may eat the fruit from any tree in the garden.

17 But you must not eat the fruit from the tree which gives the knowledge of good and evil. If you ever eat fruit from that tree, you will die!"

18 Then the Lord God said, "It is not good for the man to be alone. I will make a helper who is right for him."

19 From the ground God formed every wild animal and every bird in the sky. He brought them to the man so the man could name them. Whatever the man called each living thing, that became its name.

20 The man gave names to all the tame animals, to the birds in the sky and to all the wild animals. But Adam did not find a helper that was right for him.

21 So the Lord God caused the man to sleep very deeply. While the man was asleep, God took one of the ribs from the man's body. Then God closed the man's skin at the place where he took the rib.

22 The Lord God used the rib from the man to make a woman. Then the Lord brought the woman to the man.

23 And the man said, "Now, this is someone whose bones came from my bones. Her body came from my body. I will call her 'woman,' because she was taken out of man."

24 So a man will leave his father and mother and be united with his wife. And the two people will become one body.

Genesis 2:7-24 (International Children's Bible – ICB)

So God replaced Satan with Mankind. Needless to say this made Satan very angry, and he wanted to get back at God. So, he tricked Eve into disobeying God too.

The Fall of Man

1 Now the snake was the most clever of all the wild animals the Lord God had made. One day the snake spoke to the woman. He said, "Did God really say that you must not eat fruit from any tree in the garden?"

2 The woman answered the snake, "We may eat fruit from the trees in the garden.

3 But God told us, 'You must not eat fruit from the tree that is in the middle of the garden. You must not even touch it, or you will die.'"

4 But the snake said to the woman, "You will not die.

5 God knows that if you eat the fruit from that tree, you will learn about good and evil. Then you will be like God!"

6 The woman saw that the tree was beautiful. She saw that its fruit was good to eat and that it would make her wise. So she took some of its fruit and ate it. She also gave some of the fruit to her husband who was with her, and he ate it.

7 Then, it was as if the man's and the woman's eyes were opened. They realized they were naked. So they sewed fig leaves together and made something to cover themselves.

8 Then they heard the Lord God walking in the garden. This was during the cool part of the day.

And the man and his wife hid from the Lord God among the trees in the garden.

9 But the Lord God called to the man. The Lord said, "Where are you?"

10 The man answered, "I heard you walking in the garden. I was afraid because I was naked. So I hid."

11 God said to the man, "Who told you that you were naked? Did you eat fruit from that tree? I commanded you not to eat from that tree."

12 The man said, "You gave this woman to me. She gave me fruit from the tree. So I ate it."

13 Then the Lord God said to the woman, "What have you done?" She answered, "The snake tricked me. So I ate the fruit."

14 The Lord God said to the snake, "Because you did this, a curse will be put on you. You will be cursed more than any tame animal or wild animal. You will crawl on your stomach, and you will eat dust all the days of your life.

15 I will make you and the woman enemies to each other.

Your descendants and her descendants will be

enemies. Her child will crush your head. And you will bite his heel."

16 Then God said to the woman, "I will cause you to have much trouble when you are pregnant. And when you give birth to children, you will have great pain. You will greatly desire your husband, but he will rule over you."

17 Then God said to the man, "You listened to what your wife said. And you ate fruit from the tree that I commanded you not to eat from. "So I will put a curse on the ground. You will have to work very hard for food. In pain you will eat its food all the days of your life.

18 The ground will produce thorns and weeds for you. And you will eat the plants of the field.

19 You will sweat and work hard for your food. Later you will return to the ground. This is because you were taken from the ground. You are dust. And when you die, you will return to the dust."

20 The man named his wife Eve. This is because she is the mother of everyone who ever lived.

21 The Lord God made clothes from animal

skins for the man and his wife. And so the Lord dressed them.

22 Then the Lord God said, "Look, the man has become like one of us. He knows good and evil. And now we must keep him from eating some of the fruit from the tree of life. If he does, he will live forever."

23 So the Lord God forced the man out of the garden of Eden. He had to work the ground he was taken from.

24 God forced the man out of the garden. Then God put angels on the east side of the garden. He also put a sword of fire there.

Genesis Chapter 3:1-24 (ICB)

You see, Satan was sure that if God had kicked him out for his disobedience, then God would kick out Adam and Eve out too, and then humanity would belong to Satan. But it didn't turn out that way, because God had a plan. Humanity was given a second chance. Yes, Adam and Eve got kicked out of the Garden of Eden, but God looked after them and took care of them. He never did that for Satan or his demons, and this made Satan even madder.

Chapter 3

The Plan of Salvation in the Old Testament

In the Old Testament, the plan of Salvation was to place blood over your door, so that the death angel would pass over your household.

The Passover

1 The Lord spoke to Moses and Aaron in the land of Egypt:

2 "This month will be the first month of the year for you.

3 Both of you are to tell the whole community of Israel: On the tenth day of this month each man must get one lamb. It is for the people in his house.

4 There may not be enough people in his house

to eat a whole lamb. Then he must share it with his closest neighbor. There must be enough lamb for everyone to eat.

5 The lamb must be a one-year-old male. It must have nothing wrong with it. This animal can be either a young sheep or a young goat.

6 Keep the animal with you to take care of it until the fourteenth day of the month. On that day all the people of the community of Israel will kill these animals. They will do this as soon as the sun goes down.

7 The people must take some of the blood. They must put it on the sides and tops of the doorframes. These are the doorframes of the houses where they eat the lambs.

8 On this night they must roast the lamb over a fire. Then they must eat it with bitter herbs and bread made without yeast.

9 Do not eat the lamb raw or boiled in water. Roast the whole lamb over a fire—with its head, legs and inner organs.

10 You must not leave any of it until morning. But if any of it is left over until morning, you must burn it with fire.

11 "This is the way you must eat it: You must be fully dressed as if you were going on a trip. You must have your sandals on, and you must have your walking stick in your hand. You must eat it in a hurry. This is the Lord's Passover.

12 "That night I will go through the land of Egypt. I will kill all the firstborn of animals and people in the land of Egypt. I will punish all the gods of Egypt. I am the Lord.

13 But the blood will be a sign on the houses where you are. When I see the blood, I will pass over you. Nothing terrible will hurt you when I punish the land of Egypt.

14 "You are always to remember this day. Celebrate it with a feast to the Lord. Your descendants are to honor the Lord with this feast from now on.

15 For this feast you must eat bread made without yeast for seven days. On the first day of this feast, you are to remove all the yeast from your houses. No one should eat any yeast for the full seven days of the feast. If anyone eats yeast, then that person will be separated from Israel.

16 You are to have holy meetings on the first and last days of the feast. You must not do any work on these days. The only work you may do on these days is to prepare your meals.

17 You must celebrate the Feast of Unleavened Bread. Do this because on this very day I brought your divisions of people out of Egypt. So all of your descendants must celebrate this day. This is a law that will last from now on.

18 You are to eat bread made without yeast. Start this on the evening of the fourteenth day of the first month of your year. Eat this until the evening of the twenty-first day.

19 For seven days there must not be any yeast in your houses. Anybody who eats yeast during this time must be separated from the community of Israel. This includes Israelites and non-Israelites.

20 During this feast you must not eat yeast. You must eat bread made without yeast wherever you live."

21 Then Moses called all the elders of Israel together. He told them, "Get the animals for your families. Kill the animals for the Passover.

22 Take a branch of the hyssop plant and dip it into the bowl filled with blood. Wipe the blood on the sides and tops of the doorframes. No one may leave his house until morning.

23 The Lord will go through Egypt to kill the Egyptians. He will see the blood on the sides and tops of the doorframes. Then the Lord will pass over that house. He will not let the one who brings death come into your houses and kill you.

24 "You must keep this command. This law is for you and your descendants from now on.

25 Do this when you go to the land the Lord has promised to give to you.

26 When your children ask you, 'Why are we doing these things?'

27 you will say, 'This is the Passover sacrifice to honor the Lord. When we were in Egypt, the Lord passed over the houses of Israel. The Lord killed the Egyptians, but he saved our homes.'" So now the people bowed down and worshiped the Lord.

28 They did just as the Lord commanded Moses and Aaron.

29 At midnight the Lord killed all the firstborn sons in the land of Egypt. The firstborn of the king, who sat on the throne, died. Even the firstborn of the prisoner in jail died. Also, all the firstborn farm animals died.

30 The king, his officers and all the Egyptians got up during the night. Someone had died in every house. So there was loud crying everywhere in Egypt.

Exodus 12:1-30 (ICB)

This is the Easter story. It is also very important to understand that even then, God made a way for his people to escape the punishment of death. And just as in the Old Testament, there is also a way of escape in the New Testament. God had a plan. This time, he would send his son Jesus Christ to save us. Jesus died on the cross so that we may all live and not die.

Chapter 4

The Plan of Salvation in the New Testament

THE CRUCIFIXION OF CHRIST

Jesus Is Taken to Pilate

1 Early the next morning, all the leading priests and elders of the people decided to kill Jesus.

2 They tied him, led him away, and turned him over to Pilate, the governor.

3 *Judas saw that they had decided to kill Jesus. Judas was the one who gave Jesus to his enemies. When Judas saw what happened, he was very sorry for what he had done. So he took the 30 silver coins back to the priests and the leaders.*

4 *Judas said, "I sinned. I gave you an innocent man to be killed." The leaders answered, "What is that to us? That's your problem, not ours."*

5 So Judas threw the money into the Temple. Then he went off and hanged himself.

6 The leading priests picked up the silver coins in the Temple. They said, "Our law does not allow us to keep this money with the Temple money. This money has paid for a man's death."

7 So they decided to use the coins to buy a field called Potter's Field. This field would be a place to bury strangers who died while visiting Jerusalem.

8 That is why that field is still called the Field of Blood.

9 So the thing came true that Jeremiah the prophet had said: "They took 30 silver coins. That is how little the Israelites thought he was worth.

10 They used those 30 silver coins to buy Potter's Field, as the Lord commanded me."

Pilate Questions Jesus

11 Jesus stood before Pilate the governor. Pilate asked him, "Are you the King of the Jews?" Jesus answered, "Yes, I am."

12 When the leading priests and the elders accused Jesus, he said nothing.

13 So Pilate said to Jesus, "Don't you hear these people accusing you of all these things?"

14 But Jesus said nothing in answer to Pilate. Pilate was very surprised at this.

Pilate Tries to Free Jesus

15 Every year at the time of Passover the governor would free one person from prison. This was always a person the people wanted to be set free.

16 At that time there was a man in prison who

was known to be very bad. His name was Barabbas.

17 All the people gathered at Pilate's house. Pilate said, "Which man do you want me to free: Barabbas, or Jesus who is called the Christ?"

18 Pilate knew that they gave Jesus to him because they were jealous.

19 Pilate said these things while he was sitting on the judge's seat. While he was sitting there, his wife sent a message to him. The message said, "Don't do anything to that man. He is not guilty. Today I had a dream about him, and it troubled me very much."

20 But the leading priests and elders told the crowd to ask for Barabbas to be freed and for Jesus to be killed.

21 Pilate said, "I have Barabbas and Jesus. Which do you want me to set free for you?" The people answered, "Barabbas!"

22 Pilate asked, "What should I do with Jesus, the one called the Christ?" They all answered, "Kill him on a cross!"

23 Pilate asked, "Why do you want me to kill

him? What wrong has he done?" But they shouted louder, "Kill him on a cross!"

24 Pilate saw that he could do nothing about this, and a riot was starting. So he took some water and washed his hands in front of the crowd. Then he said, "I am not guilty of this man's death. You are the ones who are causing it!"

25 All the people answered, "We will be responsible. We accept for ourselves and for our children any punishment for his death."

26 Then Pilate freed Barabbas. Pilate told some of the soldiers to beat Jesus with whips. Then he gave Jesus to the soldiers to be killed on a cross.

27 Pilate's soldiers took Jesus into the governor's palace. All the soldiers gathered around Jesus.

28 They took off his clothes and put a red robe on him.

29 Then the soldiers used thorny branches to make a crown. They put this crown of thorns on Jesus' head. They put a stick in his right hand. Then the soldiers bowed before Jesus and made fun of him. They said, "Hail, King of the Jews!"

30 They spit on Jesus. Then they took his stick

and hit him on the head many times. **31** After they finished making fun of Jesus, the soldiers took off the robe and put his own clothes on him again. Then they led Jesus away to be killed on a cross.

Jesus Is Killed on a Cross

32 The soldiers were going out of the city with Jesus. They forced another man to carry the cross to be used for Jesus. This man was Simon, from Cyrene.

33 They all came to the place called Golgotha. (Golgotha means the Place of the Skull.)

34 At Golgotha, the soldiers gave Jesus wine to drink. This wine was mixed with gall. He tasted the wine but refused to drink it.

35 The soldiers nailed Jesus to a cross. They threw lots to decide who would get his clothes.

36 The soldiers sat there and continued watching him.

37 They put a sign above Jesus' head with the charge against him written on it. The sign read: "THIS IS JESUS THE KING OF THE JEWS."

38 Two robbers were nailed to crosses beside Jesus, one on the right and the other on the left.

39 People walked by and insulted Jesus. They shook their heads,

40 saying, "You said you could destroy the Temple and build it again in three days. So save yourself! Come down from that cross, if you are really the Son of God!"

41 The leading priests, the teachers of the law, and the Jewish elders were also there. These men made fun of Jesus

42 and said, "He saved other people, but he can't save himself! People say he is the King of Israel! If he is the King, then let him come down now from the cross. Then we will believe in him.

43 He trusts in God. So let God save him now, if God really wants him. He himself said, 'I am the Son of God.'"

44 And in the same way, the robbers who were being killed on crosses beside Jesus also insulted him.

Jesus Dies

45 At noon the whole country became dark. This darkness lasted for three hours.

46 About three o'clock Jesus cried out in a loud voice, "Eli, Eli, lama sabachthani?" This means, "My God, my God, why have you left me alone?"

47 Some of the people standing there heard this. They said, "He is calling Elijah."

48 Quickly one of them ran and got a sponge. He filled the sponge with vinegar and tied it to a stick. Then he used the stick to give the sponge to Jesus to drink from it.

49 But the others said, "Don't bother him. We want to see if Elijah will come to save him."

50 Again Jesus cried out in a loud voice. Then he died.

51 Then the curtain in the Temple split into two pieces. The tear started at the top and tore all the way down to the bottom. Also, the earth shook and rocks broke apart.

52 The graves opened, and many of God's people who had died were raised from death.

53 They came out of the graves after Jesus was raised from death. They went into the holy city, and many people saw them.

54 The army officer and the soldiers guarding Jesus saw this earthquake and everything else that happened. They were very frightened and said, "He really was the Son of God!"

55 Many women were standing at a distance from the cross, watching. These were women who had followed Jesus from Galilee to care for him.

56 Mary Magdalene, and Mary the mother of James and Joseph, and the mother of James and John were there.

Jesus Is Buried

57 That evening a rich man named Joseph came to Jerusalem. He was a follower of Jesus from the town of Arimathea.

58 Joseph went to Pilate and asked to have Jesus' body. Pilate gave orders for the soldiers to give it to Joseph.

59 Then Joseph took the body and wrapped it in a clean linen cloth.

60 He put Jesus' body in a new tomb that he had cut in a wall of rock. He rolled a very large stone to block the entrance of the tomb. Then Joseph went away.

61 Mary Magdalene and the other woman named Mary were sitting near the tomb.

The Tomb of Jesus Is Guarded

62 That day was the day called Preparation Day. The next day, the leading priests and the Pharisees went to Pilate.

63 They said, "Sir, we remember that while that liar was still alive he said, 'After three days I will rise from death.'

64 So give the order for the tomb to be guarded closely till the third day. His followers might come and steal the body. Then they could tell the people that he has risen from death. That lie would be even worse than the first one."

65 Pilate said, "Take some soldiers and go guard the tomb the best way you know."

66 So they all went to the tomb and made it safe from thieves. They did this by sealing the stone in the entrance and then putting soldiers there to guard it.

Matthew 27:1-66 (ICB)

But Don't worry, Jesus didn't stay dead. He kept telling them that he would rise again on the third day and he did.

Jesus Rises from The Grave

1 The day after the Sabbath day was the first day of the week. At dawn on the first day, Mary Magdalene and another woman named Mary went to look at the tomb.

2 At that time there was a strong earthquake. An angel of the Lord came down from heaven. The angel went to the tomb and rolled the stone away from the entrance. Then he sat on the stone.

3 He was shining as bright as lightning. His clothes were white as snow.

4 The soldiers guarding the tomb were very frightened of the angel. They shook with fear and then became like dead men.

5 The angel said to the women, "Don't be afraid. I know that you are looking for Jesus, the one who was killed on the cross.

6 But he is not here. He has risen from death as he said he would. Come and see the place where his body was.

7 And go quickly and tell his followers. Say to them: 'Jesus has risen from death. He is going into Galilee. He will be there before you. You will see him there.'" Then the angel said, "Now I have told you."

8 The women left the tomb quickly. They were afraid, but they were also very happy. They ran to tell Jesus' followers what had happened.

9 Suddenly, Jesus met them and said, "Greetings." The women came up to Jesus, took hold of his feet, and worshiped him.

10 Then Jesus said to them, "Don't be afraid. Go and tell my brothers to go on to Galilee. They will see me there."

The Soldiers Report to the Jewish Leaders

11 The women went to tell Jesus' followers. At the same time, some of the soldiers who had been guarding the tomb went into the city. They went to tell the leading priests everything that had happened.

12 Then the priests met with the Jewish elders and made a plan. They paid the soldiers a large amount of money.

13 They said to the soldiers, "Tell the people that Jesus' followers came during the night and stole the body while you were asleep.

14 If the governor hears about this, we will satisfy him and save you from trouble."

15 So the soldiers kept the money and obeyed the priests. And that story is still spread among the Jews even today.

Jesus Talks to His Followers

16 The eleven followers went to Galilee. They went to the mountain where Jesus told them to go.

17 On the mountain they saw Jesus and worshiped him. But some of them did not believe that it was really Jesus.

18 Then Jesus came to them and said, "All power in heaven and on earth is given to me.

19 So go and make followers of all people in the world. Baptize them in the name of the Father and the Son and the Holy Spirit.

20 Teach them to obey everything that I have told you. You can be sure that I will be with you always. I will continue with you until the end of the world."

Matthew 28:1-20 (ICB)

Now I know what you're thinking. That all happened thousands of years ago. What has that got to do with me now? Well, Jesus gave us this parable...

Chapter 5

The Parable of the Lost Son

11 Then Jesus said, "A man had two sons.

12 The younger son said to his father, 'Give me my share of the property.' So the father divided the property between his two sons.

13 Then the younger son gathered up all that was his and left. He traveled far away to another country. There he wasted his money in foolish living.

14 He spent everything that he had. Soon after that, the land became very dry, and there was no rain. There was not enough food to eat anywhere in the country. The son was hungry and needed money.

15 So he got a job with one of the citizens there. The man sent the son into the fields to feed pigs.

16 The son was so hungry that he was willing

to eat the food the pigs were eating. But no one gave him anything.

17 The son realized that he had been very foolish. He thought, 'All of my father's servants have plenty of food. But I am here, almost dying with hunger.

18 I will leave and return to my father. I'll say to him: Father, I have sinned against God and against you.

19 I am not good enough to be called your son. But let me be like one of your servants.'

20 So the son left and went to his father.

"While the son was still a long way off, his father saw him coming. He felt sorry for his son. So the father ran to him, and hugged and kissed him.

21 The son said, 'Father, I have sinned against God and against you. I am not good enough to be called your son.'

22 But the father said to his servants, 'Hurry! Bring the best clothes and put them on him. Also, put a ring on his finger and sandals on his feet.

23 And get our fat calf and kill it. Then we can have a feast and celebrate!

24 My son was dead, but now he is alive again! He was lost, but now he is found!' So they began to celebrate.

Luke 15:11-24 (International Children's Bible – ICB)

Do you see the correlation? Humanity is like the second son that wanted his cake and to eat it too. But all we did was squander all the precious things that had been given to us. And just like the second son, we must come to our senses and realize that we have done wrong and that we need to repent. Until, we do. We will see nothing wrong with how we are living. We will see nothing more of what we could be, which is the rightful heirs of God. Satan has lured us away with riotous living. And until we realize that we need God, we will continue wallowing in our pigsty of sin.

Chapter 6

The Plan of Salvation for You

So, how do we get back to where we need to be with God? How do we once again reclaim our inheritance with God? All you have to do is heed Acts 2:38.

Acts 2:38 says *"Then Peter said unto them, Repent, and be Baptized every one of you in the name of Jesus Christ for the remission of sins, and ye shall receive the gift of the Holy Ghost."*

Jesus and Nicodemus

1 There was a man named Nicodemus who was one of the Pharisees. He was an important Jewish leader.

2 One night Nicodemus came to Jesus. He said,

"Teacher, we know that you are a teacher sent from God. No one can do the miracles you do, unless God is with him."

3 Jesus answered, "I tell you the truth. Unless you are born again, you cannot be in God's kingdom."

4 Nicodemus said, "But if a man is already old, how can he be born again? He cannot enter his mother's body again. So how can he be born a second time?"

5 But Jesus answered, "I tell you the truth. Unless you are born from water and the Spirit, you cannot enter God's kingdom.

6 A person's body is born from his human parents. But a person's spiritual life is born from the Spirit.

7 Don't be surprised when I tell you, 'You must all be born again.'

8 The wind blows where it wants to go. You hear the wind blow. But you don't know where the wind comes from or where it is going. It is the same with every person who is born from the Spirit."

9 Nicodemus asked, "How can all this be possible?"

10 Jesus said, "You are an important teacher in Israel. But you still don't understand these things?

11 I tell you the truth. We talk about what we know. We tell about what we have seen. But you don't accept what we tell you.

12 I have told you about things here on earth, but you do not believe me. So surely you will not believe me if I tell you about the things of heaven!

13 The only one who has ever gone up to heaven is the One who came down from heaven—the Son of Man.

14 "Moses lifted up the snake in the desert. It is the same with the Son of Man. The Son of Man must be lifted up too.

15 Then everyone who believes in him can have eternal life.

16 "**For God loved the world so much that he gave his only Son. God gave his Son so that whoever believes in him may not be lost, but have eternal life.**

17 God did not send his Son into the world to

judge the world guilty, but to save the world through him.

18 He who believes in God's Son is not judged guilty. He who does not believe has already been judged guilty, because he has not believed in God's only Son.

19 People are judged by this fact: I am the Light from God that has come into the world. But men did not want light. They wanted darkness because they were doing evil things.

20 Everyone who does evil hates the light. He will not come to the light because it will show all the evil things he has done.

21 But he who follows the true way comes to the light. Then the light will show that the things he has done were done through God."

John 3:1-21 (ICB)

Jesus and Nicodemus

Baptized – Born of the Water

Receiving the Holy Ghost – Born of the Spirit

Having read all this, I am hoping that you will begin to understand how important your soul is. And how importantly God values you. He gave his life for you.

You must also understand that God loves you and cares for you whether you believe in him or not. He stands at the door of your heart and knocks.

Revelations 3:20 (ICB)

20 "Here I am! I stand at the door and knock. If anyone hears my voice and opens the door, I will come in and eat with him. And he will eat with me."

God gives us so many chances to hear his voice, open up our hearts, and obey his word. The Holy Bible is his word and every time we read it, He speaks to us. He tells us about his love for us. He tells us about how we are to live our lives. He gives us solutions to our problems. If we would just keep our eyes on him, let go of our hurt and anger, and bend our knees in prayer; then He will fight our battles for us. He will save us from our enemies. He will make ways of escape from our bills and debts. He will bring people into our lives that will enrich us and take people out of our lives that mean us nothing but harm. Open your eyes and see the goodness of The Lord.

A Good Way to Live

1 Happy is the person who doesn't listen to the

wicked. He doesn't go where sinners go. He doesn't do what bad people do.

2 He loves the Lord's teachings. He thinks about those teachings day and night.

3 He is strong, like a tree planted by a river. It produces fruit in season. Its leaves don't die. Everything he does will succeed.

Psalms 1:1-3 (ICB)

God wants you to succeed. He wants you to live with him forever in Heaven. Heed his words, answer his call, and give your life to Jesus.

Other Books by Author

60 Christian Traits
   Basics of Christianity
   Parody of Parables
   Small Fry Tales
   The Brave Little Bottle
   Toothache at Big Mouth Bend
   Cavities of the Caribbean
   Tale of Two Teeth
   Toothtown Football

www.ingramcontent.com/pod-product-compliance
Lightning Source LLC
Chambersburg PA
CBHW041320110526
44591CB00021B/2850